D0291280

# When Foxes
# Wore Red Vests

# When Foxes Wore Red Vests

## Bruce Hopkins

with pencil drawings by
## Barry Hopkins

Bruce (left) and Barry Hopkins

Ice Cube Books
North Liberty, Iowa

When Foxes Wore Red Vests:
Finding my sense of place

ISBN 9781888160468

Library of Congress Control Number: 2010921463

Ice Cube Books, LLC (est. 1993)
205 North Front Street
North Liberty, Iowa 52317-9302
www.icecubepress.com
steve@icecubepress.com

The paper used in this publication meets the minimum requirements of the American National Standard for Information Sciences—Permanence of Paper for Printed Library Materials, ANSI Z39.48-1992

Cover drawings by Bruce Hopkins
Cover design by Steve Semken

Pencil drawings by Barry Hopkins are
from the collections of:
-Karen Hopkins
-Ashley Hopkins Benton
-Bruce and Jeanette Hopkins
-Mr. and Mrs. Mark Mechlowitz
-Mr. and Mrs. Robert Lauillard
-Mr. and Mrs. Walter Janeway

The Saga of Dick and Jane was first published in Social Anarchism No. 14 , p. 65-7, 1989

# Special Thanks...

—Jeanette Hopkins, my life partner/soul mate whose wisdom and insights over the many years have resulted in the publication of this book.

—Karen Hopkins, for her sensitivity, enlightenment and support for this project.

—Paula Horii, whose background in English, writing, and literature guided our work through all of the final readings.

—Howard Horii, for his patience in discussions and the beautiful watercolor painting of the one-room schoolhouse.

—Heather Fields, for her preparation of the essays and poems.

—Ashley Hopkins Benton, for her research and guidance on issues concerning the life, and work of her father, Barry Hopkins.

—Drew Hopkins, for his environmental and educational contributions.

—Gladys Hopkins, for her lifelong commitment to her children, all things concerning family, folk myths, and stories of the Glenford Woods.

—Howard Hopkins Jr., for his technical sketch of the Catskills, Glenford Woods, Ashokan Reservoir, and place names.

—Susie (Dawn Hopkins) Axon, a wonderful sister and patron of the Glenford Methodist Church.

# Contents—

## I. Introduction                                          3

Reflections on a Sense of Place


## II. Place                                                11

Glenford Woods                                           13

The Hemlock Grove                                        20

The Den Tree                                             29

Bluestone Symmetry                                       37

When Foxes Wore Red Vests                                41

Old Route 28                                             49


## III. People                                             55

My Father's Garden                                       57

Deer Hunting                                             63

Grandfather Gray and the Copperhead                      72

Mountain Women                                           76

Maggie Drew                                              84


## IV. A Sense of Place                                    90

The One Room School


## Dedication                                             106

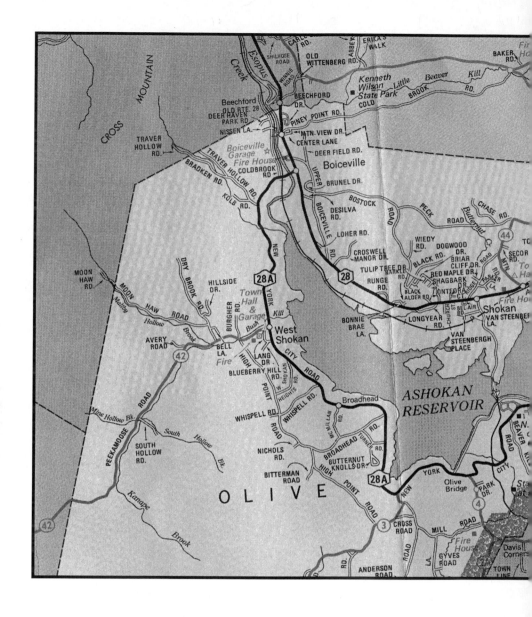

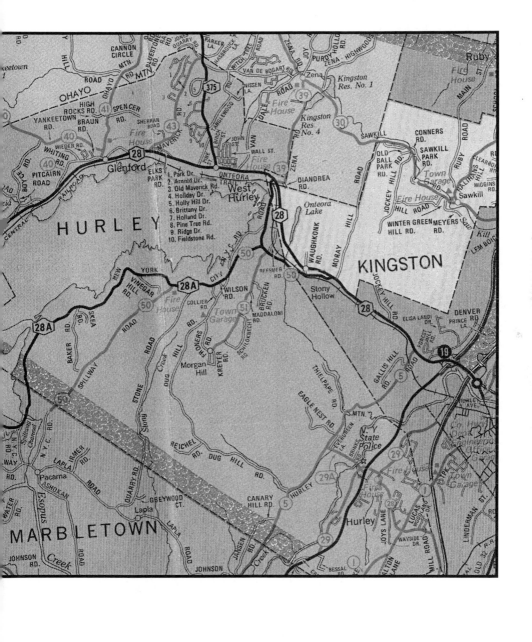

Pencil drawing by Barry Hopkins

# When Foxes
# Wore Red Vests

Pencil drawing by Barry Hopkins

# Introduction:
# Reflections on a Sense of Place

One of the most perplexing issues of our age is to reflect on when it was, and why it was, that our society began to disconnect from the natural world. As a young adult, when I first read Aldo Leopold's[1] *A Sand County Almanac*, which examined a land use ethic where the sanctity of life for humans was inextricably woven with that of every species, I began to understand the necessity of being part of the entire universe. Our wildness, in terms of personal well-being and as a species, depended on a deeper intimacy and understanding of the welfare of the entire planet.

As a child of a tightly knit extended mountain family, my early private world played out in the rural environment of a small community in the Catskill Mountains of upstate New York. In the mountains, when you meet someone for the first time, you inquire about "who" they are and "where" they are from. There is a need in this sense of "being from somewhere", of places defined by geography, topography, and the complexities of character that represent a spiritual home and place where memory and thought reside. Where I'm from is a reflection of the stories, myths and experiences of that "place."

Later, as I became familiar with the literature of other "places," it became easy to imagine, when standing on the banks of the Dismal River in Nebraska, the old cattle drives, the horse and rider crossing flooded rivers filled with quicksand as told by western writer Zane Grey.[2] It is also not difficult to envision the "characters" who populated saloons in Deadwood, South Dakota, where violence and the harshness of the climate dictated

---

1 **Aldo Leopold (1887-1948)** American conservationist, teacher, philosopher and writer.
2 **Zane Grey (1872-1939)** American writer, considered to be the father of the modern American western novel.

the frontier myths. The mountain lions of the Black Hills give credence to the austerity of the remote wild places, as well as the beauty, attending to the violence supposed in that environment. In such wild places, however, the native voices spoke to the wisdom of protecting and examining "place" as in the readings from *Black Elk Speaks,* by John Neihardt.[3]

Hundreds of miles away, where the ridgeline of the Catskill Mountains take on the most feminine and sensuous of forms, I came to know the similar messages from New England. Pastoral paintings by Thomas Cole[4] and Frederick Edwin Church[5] and all of the other Hudson River School of Artists,[6] defined this place as *Nature's Paintbrush,* depicting the myths of Pan and the landscape images as ones of majesty and honor. But, as in the West, these softening images can easily be replaced by Washington Irving's[7] tales of headless horsemen, galloping along narrow, winding roads enveloped by overhanging trees. As a small child, scurrying home through the forests at night, where shadows enliven the imagination and the baby scream of the bobcat stretches beyond the stature of this small animal, I came to know the intrigue of Irving. Our own Spook Rock and Old Route 28 became the myth and story of the region.

The Glenford, New York, that I experienced was happenstance, a by-product of the construction of the Ashokan reservoir by the City of New York. The original town, long flooded by the water needs of millions of city dwellers, now lies in the lower basin of the Ashokan Reservoir. This "new" Glenford did not exist as a discreet community, typified by the attributes of a small Midwestern town, but rather was a collection of people whose homes, small farms, churches and post offices were scattered along Old Route 28, a road that led from the historical town of Kingston, along the

---

3 John Neihardt (1881-1973) American poet, writer, editor and philosopher.
4 Thomas Cole (1801-1848) English-born American landscape painter.
5 Frederick Edwin Church (1826-1900) American landscape painter.
6 The Hudson River School of Artists A group of 19th century American landscape painters depicting pastoral settings.
7 Washington Irving (1783-1859) American author, essayist, biographer and historian.

Esopus Creek, to the resorts and ski lodges that housed the summer and winter visitors from the city.

The new Glenford provided a myriad of rich opportunities for exploration and reflection. The abandoned cemeteries, logging roads and bluestone cellars became artifacts of the expansion of the Ashokan Reservoir and led me through the history of this place and an understanding of past indiscretions caused by the completion of the water byways and new industrial interstates. Intellectually, I came to understand that the building of the reservoir, on the heels of Teddy Roosevelt's[8] initiative to create a system of National Parks and the future protection of water and land and eventual standards for the quality of both, was necessitated by the over populating of a country. But, spiritually, I also understood the destruction and distrust, still evident in the mountains today, came at a very high personal cost.

As a young child, my playground was a heavily forested area where families lived on the boundaries of this water. Boundary borders were posted by the City of New York, but my father's family had been wise enough to obtain early fishing permits that guaranteed some level of coexistence with the reservoir itself. It took years for the water supply property to return to a wild state and for natural restoration to occur, but due to the foresight of architectural figures such as Frederick Law Olmstead[9] and naturalist John Burroughs,[10] the historical and natural relationships fostered a mutual respect. Both understood the need for the human species to connect continually with nature and to take care to protect that relationship itself.

My childhood in the woods and with nature supported a bonded relationship which nurtured me. Just prior to his death in 2008, my

---

8 **Theodore Roosevelt (1858-1919)** 26th President of the United States, historian, biographer, hunter, naturalist and orator.

9 **Frederick Law Olmsted (1822-1903)** Considered the father of American landscape architecture.

10 **John Burroughs (1837-1921)** American naturalist and essayist.

younger artist brother, Barry Hopkins, wrote to me about the sense of awe that we experience as we view nature and the absolute necessity of that experience. When I visit Glenford, cresting the Ohayo mountain road from Woodstock, the lower basin of the Ashokan Reservoir unfolds in the foreground, fronted by the community of Glenford and much of the Glenford Woods. This vista is illustrative of the beauty common to the Catskills, embracing all of the communities of the Ashokan Reservoir, both natural and man-made. Mountain meadows and forests coexist with small acreages and carefully placed stone walls in the magnificent panorama laid out before the eye. I have experienced such awe in many natural settings in America, from New England, to the Sandhills of Nebraska, to the Black Hills of South Dakota and the Loess Hills of Iowa, where my wife, children's author Jeanette Hopkins, and I now live. As our language and impulses come from nature, so does our sense of beauty, empathy and affection.

Mountain people hear conversations in shadows, conch horns and the barking of dogs. I listened to Gary Synder[11] speak of walking mountains, and have heard native people articulate the need to listen to the earth. John Neihardt wrote in *Black Elk Speaks* of sacred voices. There is a deep alienation we experience when separated from nature, working in self-devised cubicles and being held captive by our own technology. Our current safety and security fears are endemic to the times in which we live, just as our education is parceled out with standards and benchmarks to be weighed and measured. Our material world, where ownership and control creates rigid boundaries, shuts some people out and treats the natural world as a set of boundless resources to be developed and exploited.

For those who have lived in mountains, near streams, swamps and forests; for those who swam in the crystal clear waters, drinking directly from them; for those who built hideouts in secretive places; for those who dammed small streams, for those carried and stocked pools with

---

11 **Gary Snyder (1930-)** American poet, essayist, lecturer and environmentalist.

pan fish, crayfish, and bullheads; for those who laid upon the earth atop dense mosses, for those who cherish fall leaves near stone walls, you were involved in the most intimate conversations. Your experiences connected each generation with the continuity of disturbances of place. What Sylvan T. Runkel[12] referred to as "citizens of the natural world."

Through a collection of my own essays, poems and journal entries and through pencil drawings by my late brother, Barry Hopkins, I hope to share with the reader a sobering, yet whimsical, reflection on the loss of innocence and the importance of engaging children in the natural world.

In a time when there is a deep alienation from the natural world, it is ever more important for children to understand the sanctity of all life and to understand a "citizens of the natural world" moral ethic.

---

12 **Sylvan T. Runkel (1906-1995)** American naturalist, teacher, conservationist, pilot, musician and co-author of wildflower guides.

# Confluence

Come with me to a quiet place
Different from the ones you have known
Where dogwoods bloom in pink and white
And the earth smells like the dew
On a fresh melon in early spring

The sounds are of the birds
And of the creaking of old trees supported by saplings
Where the slant of the sun turns specks of dust
Into a diorama
Suspended in believability

Once the tracks of a doe heavy with an unborn fawn
Impress the heart with the warmth of knowing
Creating forgiving boundaries
And tactile interludes

In the evening bats dissect
The protective overlay of blackness
Flitting in pursuit of insects
Washed with the gaze of a great horned owl
And the predictive call of a whippoorwill

Never alone
Interspersed with the vibrancy of the living
The dead and those not yet born
The sound of nature and those metaphysical forces
Which establish tranquility
If you tread softly

Bending the branches as you walk
Stepping carefully on conveniently placed damp leaves
We will together experience the pulse of the universe
Personal renewal and become as one

# Place

Pencil drawing by Barry Hopkins

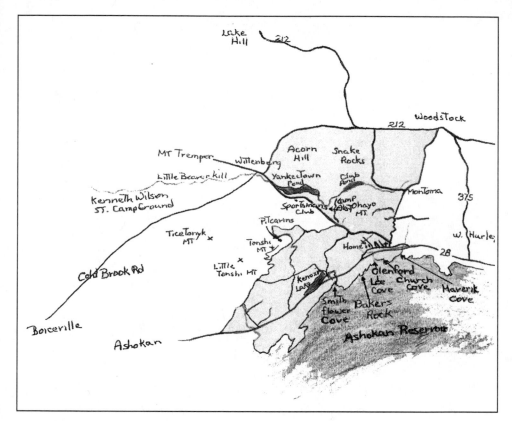

Drawing by Howard Hopkins, Jr.

# Place: Glenford Woods

As distinct as the study of the human body, an examination of Glenford Woods rivals the intimacy with nature that was offered to me, my siblings, and a limited number of mountain families in the Catskill Mountains of New York. Glenford was a small community of houses spread across the face of the Ohayo Mountain, Old Route 28, and along several roads to Woodstock and the Catskill Mountains. The north boundary was the crest of the Ohayo Mountain, from which there is a majestic view of Glenford and the lower basin of the Ashokan Reservoir.

The Ohayo Mountain served as the backdrop of our home on the southern flank of the mountain, butting up against the southern boundary formed by Old Route 28, the Ulster-Delaware Railroad tracks, and the Ashokan Reservoir. As we grew into our teens, our definition of hunting and fishing communities extended into the village of Wittenberg, the extended Catskill Mountains, and Yankee Town Pond. In the bowl of the mountains northwest of the Ohayo Mountain there was a summer camp for the disadvantaged children from New York City who engaged in physical activities with the equally disadvantaged children of the mountains. Each summer their small marching band preceded the Glenford/West Hurley Fire Department during parades in Kingston, New York, the nearest city on the Hudson River. The camp also served as our entry point into the swamp where we hunted deer, harvested princess pines for Christmas wreaths, encountered snowshoe hares, and for moments in time, became quite lost. Here our boundaries of wildness expanded, with the ever visible signs of logging decades past and the trails in the swamp strengthening our inquisitive nature and identification over time with place (Camp Alert, Wittenberg Yankee Town Pond, and the Sawmill Dam).

From our backyard, we could look up at the cliffs and rocky outcropping on the brow of the Ohayo Mountain named affectionately by the locals as High Rocks. I greeted many a morning shouting at the mountain and delighted in being greeted back by the echo of my own voice. Standing in the middle of Old Route 28 (which served as our route to anywhere— our playground, our baseball field, sled run, bicycle route and race car track), I could see the white building of the Pitcairn Estate. Tonshi Peak was the home of the estate overlooking our community, a reminder of the extreme circumstances of folk who inhabited this region and the far different worlds in which they lived and their mutual dependency. This mountain drew me in at the same time as the swamp and mountains at Wittenberg. The Ohayo Mountain peak served as the north boundary of the Glenford Woods and Tonshi Peak was at the west end.

Below the Pitcairn Estate on the west end of Glenford was a small mountain lake called Temple's Pond (now signed as Kenozia Lake). This pond bordered New Route 28 and is also represented in the Glenford Woods and the town of Ashokan. Unlike Yankee Town Pond in Wittenberg, which was bordered by many different property owners, Temple's Pond was a private property and largely ignored in my explorations. The Pitcairn family did support the Glenford Fire Department of which my father, Howard Hopkins, was a founding member and served for a while as the Fire Chief. They had also provided most of the funding for the acquisition of a four-wheel drive fire truck, (following a large fire at the Pitcairn Estate), in which the heavy snow had prevented the existing fire trucks from negotiating close to the fire.

The eastern edge of Glenford was defined by Route 28 and the community of West Hurley. The communities of West Hurley, Ashokan, and Glenford all bordered the lower basin of the Ashokan Reservoir. They shared pastors in the Methodist Church and joined the Onteora Central School, founded in the late fifties. Along Route 28, two rock cuts formed the dividing line between the Glenford Woods and West Hurley. Route 28 directed traffic east towards Kingston and the Hudson River, then two hours south to New York City. Remnants of Old Route 28 ran south of these cuts. At this point, the roads were well preserved and served as access points to trails leading to the Ashokan Reservoir a few hundred yards away.

My childhood experiences began in 1941 when I was born and continued until I left for college two decades later. Glenford was not so isolated from other communities such as Woodstock, which is considered the Greenwich Village of the Catskills. Many of my ancestors are buried in the Artists' Cemetery in Woodstock. Many mountain men and women were artisans, building wonderful stonewall fences, creating beauty in the gardens of families who recreated in the mountains. Whoever resided in the Catskill Mountains—Washington Irving,[1] Pete Seeger,[2] The Hudson River School of Artists[3]—felt the topography speak to them.

When I visit with the friends who knew me then, we talk about how two conditions colored our lives. One was the freedom to explore our environment and the other was the development of a personal conservation ethic. I could emulate Henry David Thoreau[4] wandering where feet took me without meeting another person for miles. I could cross unmarked property lines and become part of a community of flora and fauna. I found solace in the wind and the continuity of a mountain stream. Children of the mountains were often without supervision, as supervised activities often bore the brunt of punishment that was never questioned. Finding our own voices required that we break away, that we experience the mountains in our own way, and learn to thrive in that aloneness.

---

1 **Washington Irving (1783-1859)** American author, essayist, biographer and historian.

2 **Pete Seeger (1919-)** American folksinger and environmentalist.

3 **The Hudson River School of Artists** A group of 19th century American landscape painters depicting pastoral settings.

4 **Henry David Thoreau (1817-1862)** American writer, philosopher and naturalist.

# Catskill Mountain Allegory

Echoes of primitive drums and ancient rituals
Somber darkened rings of blue green cedar
Carried on the winds of chaotic breezes
Sounds of horses harnessed against stone cold sledges

Mountain laurel of unrepentant beauty
Slipped on the steps of ledges
Furtive suggestive tumbling clouds
Shadows of quiescent bobcats and introspective ferns

Slipping through of the hunting owl
The ghost-like presence of white-tailed deer
Intertwining strands of massive grapevines
Pastoral epiphany

# Sphinx Moth-The Dance

In the outline of faeries
dancing in the early morning dew...
catching the rays at day's end
splashing midst shadows
on the refractions of a discerning eye,
The sphinx moth hangs and darts.

Somewhere many worlds away
a stone faced sphinx
supports that fancy...
Is not a part of being,
but of the frenzy
of things subdued.

Art is ephemeral.
Beauty dashes on its own accord...
We bring to these delicacies
the eyes that faeries
have anointed.

These eyes know your form
as a set of feelings...
Basking in the underglow
of being a part with
the faeries...the sphinx moth
of an eternal dance.

# Artist Cemetery/Woodstock N.Y.

In this grassy
Ant infested rock place
They lay in earthy solitude
Familiar family names
Commemorating kinships
And spots on the mountains
That bore their names

Sometimes the flower children
Of a more modern age
Smoked pot and mocked eternity
Wilted flowers dried with the passing
Of a summer breeze
Blue jays raucously proclaimed
The passing of another day

Rutted rock gutted road
Passed among the weeds
And rumbled on the bottom side of cars
Dandelions decayed on to smoke
Black-eyed Susans stood repentant
Against the stark outline of crosses
And the images of prostrate lambs

Tears welled, crept, and disarranged
On the mapping of sun parched skin
Veins protruded on crusted hands
Outlining a celebration
Of ages spent
And lives that crossed
Intermittently

Pencil drawing by Barry Hopkins

# Place: The Hemlock Grove

The Hemlock Grove, north, up the hill from our house was home to whippoorwills, red and grey squirrels, and creatures whose woodland voices characterized their presence.

Between our house and the grove was a small plot of land which served as a family garden. Once a year a farmer from the area would bring his pair of draft horses and plow the land. He was a coarse and determined man. He set himself apart from his neighbors as he contented himself with plowing and farming which he knew best. As with many New England natives, he mixed the color of his language with the hard life he knew and then with the lives of his wife and other souls who spent their time in the good works of the local and only church.

Up the hill from the garden was a hillside which had been logged. The old stumps served as a convenient backrest for conversation. The south of the grove was set apart by a new growth timber of mixed woods: maple, ashes, tulip trees, and iron wood growth. This was an ideal place from which to cut poles that could be fashioned into bows and arrows, or fishing rods.

This mixed forest was outlined by a stone wall. Inside the woods the area was bushy, bordering Old Route 28. It did not have elements to support grey or red squirrels. Occasionally, I would chase out a rabbit. It was an area which was difficult to travel. The floor was rocky, at best, and what trail there was might accommodate a beagle, but not comfortably. A youthful hunter such as myself, competing with the early setting sun, found little reason to stay.

The north wood border was outlined by a small stream. Along the boundaries of this stream, in every season, our lives were played out building dams, constructing rafts, hunting frogs, ice-skating, cutting pussy willows, and general exploration.

During each season, the small stream presented herself in differing ways. In winter, she would freeze over, water gurgling between the flattened rocks and boulders. The ice was translucent, honeycombed, and feathered. Spring would send the waters into the willows on its banks and into the forest. By mid-summer, the hellgrammites and crayfish would be exposed to the sensing fingers of young boys. All along its route sacred places were defined by the building of huts, various boyhood initiations rites, and contemplation. The lives of mountain children involved deep conversation for the purpose of playful enterprise. The endless task was trying to find sense in a world inhabited by adults and then move on to the more important life activities.

The hemlock grove, even in the most windy of conditions, allowed a quiet which only nature could orchestrate. Each creature would become distinctive, both in its role and behavior. Crows called from cliffs high on the mountain. At night, the call of bobcats imitated that of babies crying and they hurried my footsteps and pulse. Owls mixed their muted voices with comments by the wind and then slid through the shadows of the hunting moon.

The northwest side of the Hemlock Grove contained a small abandoned dump. Here I found treasures—broken pieces of colored glass, a rusty toy pistol, which became a valued sidearm. It was in this Hemlock Grove that my earliest hunting expeditions gained their form. The Hemlock Grove, with its majestic canopy, forty feet above the forest floor, carpeted in needles, assisted me in walking softly to avoid exciting red squirrels and blue jays, who seemed to live in order to alert all other creatures of an unexplained presence. I practiced walking silently, sidestepping small twigs and leaves whose agitated state would betray my presence.

In my early teenage years, it was in the Hemlock Grove that I taught my cat, Elvis, to retrieve red squirrels. Elvis, whose side- burned whiskers bounced as he walked behind me, ever alert, stepping sprightly, would pounce on the prey as soon as the shot could be heard. Most he surrendered, though at times, one would be his to keep.

This was a place where the soul demanded reverence. It was in these hemlocks that I came to understand solitude and sacredness. In today's technological world, where children cannot play without some type of new device, I worry where they will go to reflect and understand connections to the natural world.

# The Stream

Frozen
Portions of it solid
Other parts
Honeycombed with soft spots

Cold, clear water
Gurgling
Beneath the ice
Entrapping
Partially decayed
Twigs and leaves

Spring thaw
Sends the stream
Out of its normal boundaries
Cleansing the system

Gradually,
As the rains become
More gentle
And the weather warms...
the stream
assumes a more leisurely pace

Slowly,
New forms appear
Frogs
Salamanders
Turtles
and snakes

In dry times,
The stream
would disappear in places

Along its route,
Small springs
sustain rivulets
seeping downward into
wet spots

Temporary haven for those creatures
requiring a wet environment

In the fall
The frogs disappear
Fresh rain
would once again
bring the stream to its banks
in a much more leisurely way
than its agitated spring condition

Leaves of oaks
maples
and sumac
carpet the surface
Ice forms in quiet places
Delicate, translucent,
unobtrusive at first,
Subtle harbinger of things to come.

Once again the weather worsens
Camouflaged by ice and snow
The stream protects
Life transposed
For the season.

Pencil drawing by Barry Hopkins

# On Finding the Hemlock Felled

When I first came to know
The smell of hemlock
To feel the needles fine
Interring chips of aged bluestone

To taste the softness of mountain women
Experiencing the sensuality of the Catskills
Awakening the senses
To the call of bluejays and scolding squirrels

The unmended stone walls
Breached by the thawing of spring and hunters
Crusty interminable lichens
Sequestered spiders' webs and rabbit havens

The tears I shed
In passing to manhood
Did not prepare me
For when they cut you down.

# Pine Forest

One imagines
That in the manger
There must have been
Pine boughs

Whose freshness
Aroma
Indicated
That nothing could
Corrupt this place

Pine needle carpet
quiet...
peaceful...
tranquil...

Partridge
Squirrels
Chipmunks
In this spot
Lose that noisy side of their nature
For which each is noted

Pine forests
Dignify

Wind and rain
Pelt down in hardwood groves
Leaves whirling to the ground
Soil eroded

Pine needle carpet
Absorbs the rain
Without a trace
Or sign of disturbance

# Place: The Den Tree

Glenford Woods was as varied and run with character as the lines on my Grandmother Gray's hand. North and west of the Hemlock Grove was a hundred year old silver maple that had been shattered by lightning, battered by the remnants of hurricanes, and tropical storms that had ascended from the Carolinas before moving onto New York/New England and then out to the sea. The earth around this ancient silver maple we called The Den Tree. The area was cluttered with large strips of bark and discarded limbs. The tree's hollow shell now stood like chimney stones marking the spot where a mountain cabin had once stood. The Den Tree was a hollow remnant and home to a clan of gray squirrels.

A small stream wound its way from the wet mountain meadows, flowing downward, past the Den Tree to the north and the Hemlock Grove to the south. As a boundary, the stream was not formidable, as a companion and staging area for a gray squirrel hunt, it represented the place where the sighting of gray squirrels first took place and the hunt began. In the fall, when squirrel season commenced, the stream lacked its rambunctious enthusiastic Spring condition. The stream was fed by a number of natural springs, so it flowed freely in all seasons. Its gurgling voice could be heard long before the stream was visible. It resembled a vein or artery connecting many communities, which together, formed Glenford Woods.

I developed an early preoccupation with slipping through brushy terrain and wooded areas, trying to leave no signs of having been there and moving as silently as possible. The route to The Den Tree involved a short walk west on Old Rout 28, before slipping into a mixed forest of ironwood, ashes and maples, probably a former wood lot. This section was best remembered for the small branches which grabbed at my hat, knapsack, gun and clothes. Here, also, was initiated the practice of displacing branches while holding them in place so as not to be whacked and disheveled when the branches rebounded. The ground underfoot was rocky, uneven and difficult to walk quietly upon. With each step I would pause, watch intently, and listen before resuming my trek. It was here that I would load my 22 Bolt Action rifle with a single 22 long rifle cartridge. The understanding that guns were dangerous, that one never carried a gun loaded on our property, in a car or along the road, was something I knew and adhered to.

Walk through the Hemlock Grove toward the Den Tree was an experience that I looked forward to even before the hunt began. The ancient hemlocks had carpeted the forest floor with needles several inches deep. Their majestic interlocking canopy, some sixty feet above the forest floor, filtered the sunlight, creating an open cathedral-like atmosphere. It was one of the few places I could imagine walking barefoot, and a place I would often go when I needed to separate myself from life's greater concerns.

It was a place where walking quietly was achievable. Even as I made my way through this natural cathedral, imagining William Cullen Bryant[1] standing there as he wrote *Inscription For The Entrance to a Wood*, the sentinels that patrol wild places had discovered my presence and would announce my arrival to the world.

Eastern red squirrels are inquisitive, noisy, small and often sounded the initial alarm by chattering rambunctiously at my presence. Flying through the lofty branches of the hemlock they would herald my arrival. I have never harbored any feelings that I was alone when outdoors.

1 **William Cullen Bryant (1794-1878)** American poet and editor.

Nearing the stream, the chickadees became active by calling each other and flitting about within reach. The raucous call of the bluejay was buttressed only by the caw of the crows.

Hunting small game was an introductory course to the larger issues of placing food on the table that underscored hunting and fishing, each in its own season. Together it was a year-round venture. The gray squirrels of the Den Tree provided a context no less filled with anticipation and wonderment than the baseball games we played. I harvested a limited number each year, being careful not to overhunt the Den Tree area. I was careful with each shot. I would take care not to destroy meat, calculating a shot to the head or the shoulder. Gray squirrels were tough, unlike rabbits that were easy to skin. The gray squirrel skin was attached to the body with a strong film, the fur itself was also tough. We would save the skins and tails, rubbing the skins with salt and attaching them to a board.

Two stories stand out in my mind that involve the hunting of gray squirrels near the Den Tree. One concerns a neighboring farmer whose family owned much of the Glenford Woods, particularly the Hemlock Grove, Mountain Meadows and the Den Tree, as well as the spring from which my family received our water for many years. (This eventually led me to a conflict with a one-room school teacher who posed the question: "Why does water run downhill?" I said, because the spring is on the mountain…the teacher held out for gravity.)

One fall afternoon while I was pursuing a gray squirrel near the Den Tree I heard the rustle of someone walking down through the woods towards me. It was the farmer. He asked me how many shots I had fired. At least one had gone through the roof of his barn and disturbed his milking. As he left, no words of anger, no warning, just a "I thought you should know" comment was issued to me.

The other story is about my trusty and sometimes hunting partner, my feline retriever, a cat named Elvis. Elvis had a black skull cap and sideburns.

Sometimes when I hunted close to home, he would follow along. The one exception to not shooting red squirrels was that I would sometimes shoot one and present it to him as a reward for the gray squirrels he retrieved.

The woods were a safe haven. I never encountered an adult I didn't know around the Den Tree and the Hemlock Grove. The woods were a natural laboratory for the study of meadows, springs, forests and stone walls. The woods provided for my family, and gave me a natural schooling that I've grown to appreciate each day since.

Pencil drawing by Barry Hopkins

# Images of Youth

Stony Hollow
Slide Mountain
Baker's Rock
Images of Youth

Scenic landscape
Autumn colors
Rocky bottomed streams

Pine needle carpets
Squirrels chattering
Crows calling
Echoes

Summer rainstorms
The first snow of winter
Deer droppings
Rabbit tracks
Clear icicles

The cove
Crayfish
Rockbass
And sunnies

Grapevine swings
Bough covered hideouts
Hidden paths
Boys 'n girls

Stonewalls

Abandoned orchards

    Restorative

    Memories

# As Leaves Fall

Leaves fall
    from autumn trees
Consulting the edge of breezes
    that the eye fails to discern

A White Pine
    causes a clutch
    in the heart
        erasing the dull ache
        associated with unending
            rows of corn

A dragonfly clung to my hand
    in association

photo taken by Ashley Hopkins Benton

# Place: Bluestone Symmetry

Glenford Woods was a collective creation of wanderings, of huts and dam building. My early hunting paths appeared on no official map and probably in no family conversation other than my own. Rural environments are sources of wonderment and intrigue. Social critics examine such places with skepticism and distrust, characterizing their inhabitants as isolated, out of touch and even ignorant. I see the rural environment as an intimate, place-based setting, whereas our current education system is skewed to accommodate an overpopulated and exploited world.

When the Ashokan Reservoir was created in the early twentieth century, the methods used for production were historical. Sledges were used to remove rock, drawn by horses, mules and oxen. Area artisans joined Italian stone cutters and African-American team drivers in the nearly ten-year construction project. Towns disappeared as the upper and lower basins filled with pure mountain water. As the city of New York, in its grave need for water, utilized eminent domain and bought up the valley lands, local folk became overwhelmed in the realization that relocation would be coming. Land buyouts seldom matched true market value.

The city of New York, in its deliberative process and in the acquisition of land, reinforced existing distrust between the people of the Catskills and their city brethren. This distrust is mirrored today by regional discussions concerning the acquisition of second homes in the Catskills and Adirondacks. As land prices are artificially elevated, mountain folk are once again displaced.

As children in the one-room schools, we were impressed when studying the pyramids of Egypt, not so much for their imposing presence, but for the dynamics and precision of their construction. Mountain folk have great familiarity with stone construction. Many quarries dotted the Ashokan Reservoir near West Hurley. Bluestone was abundant.

Of all the remnants of stone work that were left behind as folks departed the Ashokan Reservoir property, one stood out in my mind. The path to an abandoned farmstead began on old Route 28 near the Glenford church. The path continued through the New York Board of Water supply fence toward the reservoir across new Route 28 toward the church cove. Even with my limited experience, I was taken with the qualities that I could see had led this family to select this particular spot for their home. The valley that became the bed of the reservoir lay south and below them. Hardwoods of maples, hickory and ash were available everywhere. A small stream passed east of the church providing water for whatever stock the farmer raised. This was a family meticulous in the certain slant of their eye, creating a sanctuary in the midst of wildness.

As I approached the farm, carefully laid slabs of bluestone led to the foundation of the family home. The basement, lined with bluestone, held remnants of the family's quick departure. Enameled pots and broken plates competed with fallen tree limbs and leaves. Around the yard were many flowers and bushes that continued to bloom, sweet williams, lilacs, lily of the valley and wild geraniums. The greatest of all the vestiges of hard work, dedication and affection of the previous owner was the perfectly symmetrical hand-dug bluestone well. Predating the Ashokan Reservoir, the farmer had arduously used a pick ax, mattock, shovel and wedge bar to separate earth from stone. No dynamite, no mechanical devices, had assisted the family in creating one of the purest forms of man-made art. Issues arising from the building of the New York City reservoirs in the Catskills were not tidy and pastoral. The remnants of this farmstead illustrated a true labor of love.

The bluestone well was surrounded by lily of the valley, and its entrance was partially hidden from sight by a large slab of bluestone. Once I was drawn to the well, I was immediately overwhelmed by the care and the accuracy with which each stone had been set. The circular form led downward forty feet. It appeared that the measurements at the bottom would offer the same circumference as the measurements anywhere along its side. This was the work of an artisan, not a singularly utilitarian effort. Water is synonymous with life, the most basic element for survival. Its purity is a commanding necessity, particularly when cattle, sheep and fowl live in some proximity to the house. I thought of the ancient Egyptians, their precision, their amazing engineering feats. This rural farmer had moved large quantities of bluestone (the well, the walkways, the foundation of the house), painfully measuring, cutting and setting each piece.

I can't imagine that I was the only one when passing through this loveliest of properties taken with everything communicated about the people who selected this spot in the forest. The pearl in the crown was the hand-dug bluestone well. Every care had been taken for its purpose, beauty, artistry and symmetry.

It is hard to reconcile the immense loss as the family was forced to abandon their dreams, the product of years of backbreaking labor. The specter of finality when the graves of loved ones were removed (an act for which the family received a small stipend) was almost too much to bear. In spite of the decades between the time this family surrendered their property and my visit, the natural elements had been good stewards. Lily of the valley are hearty and persistent, and were spreading from the beds next to the house into the mixed hardwood forests. Blue and white lilacs grew straggly with time. Anyone who has created flower beds from the rocky soil of New York and New England knows the effort required to tame them. Using the rich matter from the henhouses and the cattle yards, mingled with the leaves of fall in natural loam, this family had obviously succeeded. Like abandoned pioneer cemeteries everywhere, where remnants of wild flowers now thrive against tilted headstones, the flowers of farmsteads dotting the Ashokan Reservoir showed a Puritan resolve and persevered.

This family and the other hearty folk who worked to create a personal Eden in the wilderness suffered greatly. Gardens, hand-dug bluestone wells and the construction of stone walls were an intensely personal undertaking. Leaving led to grieving. Families were completely uprooted during the building of the Ashokan Reservoir. Communities were flooded, bringing change to the rural mountain culture, but the wild in the Catskills gradually came back to the woodland buffer, and even to the reservoir itself.

Upper basin of the Ashokan Reservoir from the dividing weir. Photo taken by Ashley Hopkins Benton

# Place: When Foxes Wore Red Vests

During the early 1940s life in the Catskill Mountains was about stories, about listening to, telling, remembering and passing down anecdotes embellished by the wisdom of a few elders. My earliest mountain memories center around a younger brother who died of pneumonia. In those years, pneumonia claimed the lives of many and changed the fabric of mountain families forever. Temperatures would hover between 104 and 106 degrees and with penicillin not yet available, the fears of mothers were very real. My mother's alcohol sponge baths are embedded in my mind, and her terror of having a child die and of the raven's warnings, cannot be erased by intellectual ease.

The raven warning is a folk myth common to many rural mountain families (almost always women) who believe that the sight of a raven near their home foretells death. Adding to the sense of mystery, the raven is not native to the region. When I asked an older woman about the myth, she gave example after example of its reality for those who have experienced it. "When it happens to you, it's not a myth," she said.

I remember lying on a towel, the window open with a cold mountain breeze evaporating the alcohol from my body. Even now I feel the chills that wracked my body. My mother and doctor, both fighting the fever and the fear brought on by illness, caused me to reflect on the assurances I knew. As my fever worsened, I left the world of human discourse and listened instead to the pressing voice of the whippoorwill carrying me into a world populated by a red fox who wore a red vest with gold buttons and fancy blue pants.

This fox kept me alive with conversations of hemlock forests, clear mountain streams, and his stories of the woodlands. His round eyes were dark and knowing. He was clearly a dandy of sorts, the gold buttoned red vest covered an ivory shirt, the shirt adorned with gold cufflinks. His blue knickered pants reminded me later of a young English Lord, a gentry, never seen in these parts of the mountains.

His discussion with me began on the stump of the old hemlock tree and he assured me of my life. His conversation taught me to listen to the stories of the wind and to respect the talking earth. I have no idea how much time passed. It seemed indeterminable. The fox was calm, assuring, he told me not to be afraid, that I was going to be all right. Throughout, I could still hear the voice of the whippoorwill. I learned first-hand that day about the profound assurances of nature.

Upon returning from delirium, I related my observations and discussions to my mother and the doctor. It was important to them, for some reason, to make me understand that the fox wasn't real. But he was, and so were the whippoorwills whose voices from the woods lulled me to a rested sleep. These voices from deep within the mountains created a private world for the boy I was, and the man I came to be. The assurances of nature can provide us with natural guardians, true kindred spirits.

# When Foxes Wore Red Vests

Walking
Through the trepidations
of forty years

Dreams
So real that foxes wore
Red vests

Leather laced
Hunting boots
With a snap pocket
Knife

Spelling
On the steps
Of a one-roomed school
In the sunlight

Walks home through
The woods
With older girls
Whose methods
Made for a turbid soul

Working with soil
where rocks grew
To create a garden
From pine needles

Hunting in the hemlocks
And the cedar
Heavy with the dew
From a doe's eye

Athletic letters...class ring
Offered to a woman
By a boy
Too young to know
That trophies cap a season

Crying in the winter of the night

Calvinistic faith
Monastic strength
Ideas and knowledge
In conflict with one's god

Mesmerized by pitchers of beer
Warm thighs
And moist lips

Defined in a three piece suit
More cars
Than vanity can
Support

Academic certainty
Slipping away by degrees
As the numbered years glide past

# Nature's Mantra

I've never told you
Of the night deliriums
When as a child
I first trembled

In those times, fear
Kept those around me from understanding
They could not hear the prayers
    of the hemlock
Or the sacred mantra of the whippoorwill

It is instinctive to know
I have not learned from the layers of pain
    that preceded the alcohol baths of children
        the insoluble proceedings of divorce..
            and the grieving

I have listened to the voices of snow geese
    and wondered
            at the tracks of deer and wild turkey
                on fresh snow

You entered into the impressionistic mirage
    set in a field of mid-summer daisies
            framed in lines of suggestive sunlight

I did not see you in the limitations of the eye
    I could hear the voice of the hemlock

in the movements of your long skirt
          touching the bareness of your ankle
               caressed by ever attentive daisies
Caught in the embrace of nature's adoration.

# The Eternal Child

In the resonates that grandparents experience
in the trembling of the cottonwood leaves
are found those most sacred of voices
which speak not in language or intelligible words

The decoding that babies undertake
the recognition of their mother's voice…
their father's touch.
That awakens in them an acceptance of nurturing
that they in their turn may mirror that
which they have received

These sounds that first nature unveils
and which have been mimicked by respected elders
Babies searching…looking into eyes…
holding fingers…explores the eternal.

Such are the wonders that children reflect
Reminding their elders of their connections
with nature and each other.

Pencil drawing by Barry Hopkins

# Place: Old Route 28

Sometime, early in my youth, the state of New York decided it was important for people to be able to make their way to the numerous ski lodges and resorts in the Catskills without having to venture through all the small scenic byways with bothersome turns. So after a great deal of drilling and blasting the bluestone outcropping gave way to a thoroughly modern highway, New Route 28.

Old Route 28 received its character from the way in which it wound around the outline of the Northern flank of the Ashokan Reservoir and the border it provided for the Catskill Mountains. Old Route 28 assured that no one came down in a "hurried" measure. Its very narrowness, receptivity to potholes and sharp turns, allowed that only those familiar with its intricacies could speed along the route.

My father spoke in deep reverence about rides we would take on a combination of old Route 28 and new Route 28, from Glenford up along the banks of the Esopus Creek, the main tributary to the Ashokan Reservoir, going through the northern and western Catskills, the Adirondacks, and then home. Those mountains were wondrous and their beauty so incredible, that the more I saw on those Sunday drives, the greater was the attraction of the places not yet seen. In my mind, the visions of baseball immortals in Cooperstown could only compete with places like Devil's Den, Phonecia, Ash Hollow and Slide Mountain.

Old Route 28 had as much to do with my growing up as the very veins in my body. Rites of passage came to be defined by this road. Adult warnings normally included warnings to be careful of "crossing roads" and "not to go beyond the church turn." Mountain folk named every turn in the road, every hole in the fence, every notch in the mountain, each stream, and wet spot as well as all distinctive trees. I learned to read the mountains as if given a topographic map captioned in black. It came to represent my first path to somewhere, east towards the Glenford church, the post office and as I grew older, to the western Catskills and Adirondacks, and then later to college in Poughkeepsie.

Old Route 28 was our playground. On hot summer days, I would search for the tar bubbles to walk on and listen to the crisp "snap". It was along these Glenford confines that I learned to ride my bike, a light blue girl's Schwinn model that my father had bartered in return for some painting he had done. From the point at which our driveway intersected with Old Route 28, there was a gentle slope, providing a perfect hill on which to coast. Here I learned to stay upright without pedaling.

The bluestone chips which formed the gravel on the edge of the road provided the onset of many accidents and the source of scars still visible to this day. One sobering reality associated with bike riding on Old Route 28 was that the gentle hills induced a sense of courage, riding fast beyond the point of being able to pedal. Loose gravel built up on the sides of the turns, and the loss of control was irreversible. Suddenly falling, landing on my hands and knees, the bike tangled around my body, I would brace myself for the pain that would soon follow along with the inevitable cuts, bruises and ultimately, scars.

Learning to ride my bike was a lonely activity. The successes outlined in minute steps…being able to lift the push leg onto a pedal…coasting for a few feet…pedaling, turning and then eventually learning to brake. Once I learned to ride, there was a period where I would affix baseball cards with clothespins to the bike's frame. They would clack along the spokes as I raced down the road. The challenge was to arrange the cards so they would not wear out, to create new and more interesting sounds by varying the composition of the cards and the speed of the bike.

Old Route 28 served to nurture me and to provide the context for the most delicate of observations. There were sections where strawberries grew in the hard bluestone sideway, where spring violets bloomed with shortened stems, where red ants and black ants could be observed carrying out their daily activities. During winter, the old highway was a source of really good sledding hills.

After a snowfall, the town plow would come through, followed shortly by a sand truck. After the sand truck, I would work feverishly covering up the sanded spots with packed snow and begin to build the sleigh runs. Broken arms, burned legs and bloody noses blossomed from the icy track created by young warriors.

My walk to school began on Old Route 28, before turning left up the Ohayo Mountain at the Glenford Methodist Church. Even fall baseball games were played on the only flat spot on the old route. The occasional limousine drivers from New York City would sometimes interrupt our games to inquire about the best route to "somewhere else". The driver would leave with clear instructions to some unpaved notch or logging road and on we would go to pitch, and a fielder would snag down whatever eluded the team.

The south side of Old Route 28 was New York City property. Bordering the Ashokan Reservoir, the city property was contained by a four-foot fence which ran the full perimeter of the Ashokan Reservoir. The property was heavily wooded. Any foul ball which deposited itself on city property became an automatic "out". When a ball managed to find itself directly below the bottom strand of the fence it would set off severe debate among players. Poison ivy thrived in the often disturbed lines of the fence. Dodger fans could only assume that a dose of poison ivy was fit retribution for the incursion on the posted New York City property.

Old Route 28 was a windy, narrow road. White markers indicated the presence of culverts, where small streams were overlaid with pussy willows and blue flag iris. The turns were like swinging doors, creating a sense of familiarity. Paths led off old Route 28 to places like the Glenford School and the Ashokan Reservoir. It supported gravel sideways where fishermen would park, inviting anyone who came that way to stop and enter the comforting woods. New Route 28 was a thoroughfare. Gone were the conversational encounters with neighbors in the middle of the road as both stopped their cars and rolled down their windows to talk, while others passed by and waved. The initiation of new Route 28, particularly the dynamite blasting which disturbed foundations and cracked walls, was prescient. Truck traffic increased on the new road, and the railroad largely expired. It wasn't the road of familiarity anymore. It became the road to somewhere else.

Photo taken by Jeanette Hopkins

# The Nature of Community

Even with all the lacerations
    the land retained
        its fine lines.

Graveled roads
    wound among the harvested fields
    crossed the bridges of simplistic forms,
        past cemeteries
            and abandoned farmsteads.

As the population declined
    Stonewalls outlined
        a history of
        small towns and burgs.

It held on to their historic past
    and a broader sense of
        community,

Commemorated with the names
    of families whose
    descendents had moved on.

# People

Henry and Pearl Hopkins

Howard Hopkins, Sr.

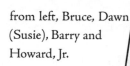

from left, Bruce, Dawn (Susie), Barry and Howard, Jr.

Gladys and Howard Hopkins (back) Glen (baby), bottom, left to right Bruce and Howard Hopkins, Jr.

# People: My Father's Garden

My father worked his fingers to the bone, as did my mother. We were raised to distrust idle time, idle hands in particular. On the weekends my father worked in the garden. I was taught to stay busy too, one of my weekend tasks was to exterminate Japanese Beetles. My least favorite method was to snap off their heads. The slight "POP" of the head was similar to the snapping of fresh green beans.

Another aggravating task was to remove the rocks from the flower garden. Using a small fruit basket I would harvest the rocks and throw them over the bank in the front yard. This created one of life's great mysteries that I have often pondered. Even though I carefully removed the pebbles and larger rocks which made their way into the garden, the very next morning it would look like someone had come in the middle of the night and salted the earth with rocks of every size and character. Despite my efforts at removing rock, and the tedious task of enriching the soil with leaves and mulch, and even placing carp under the rose bushes all was for naught. Until the bitter end, the garden sported more rocks than soil.

I would puzzle over my father's love of work. On the hottest summer days, he could be found working in his garden, wearing a white, sleeveless t-shirt. His rows were formed with purpose. The holes he dug for roses were perfect, and the technique predictable. He was methodical in his preparation for planting roses. A shovel, mattock, pick ax and pry bar were necessary to loosen the earth and remove the rocks so that a hole could be dug. Once it was dug, the bottom was filled with a mixture of compost, soil and fertilizer. He would trim the roots with a pair of clippers, pulling them outward before pushing the rose down over and into the prepared soil. Then the hole was filled with water to aerate the soil and provide nutrients to the new bush. It was then filled with soil up to the nub of the bush. A slight mounding of loose soil was created around the circumference of the bush to provide an indentation for additional watering. The soil near the top of the plant was dressed with "mushroom soil" we got from the extensive mushroom caves near Kingston. While others might have used the substances available from their small farming operations, the secret ingredient for fertilizing my father's garden was this mushroom soil he bought from the growers in the Kingston flats near Hurley where we also went to buy annuals.

He prided himself on his variety of Jackson-Perkins roses. In the fall, the bushes were severely trimmed back, mounded for protection and often covered with fruit baskets. In spite of the harshness of Catskill winters, he lost very few plants. While we were young, tending the garden was listed among our chores. He would mix a somewhat predictable variety of flowering plants—potted plants, geraniums, mums, perennials, black-eyed Susans, daisies, roses, pansies, crocus, tulips and gladiola bulbs. The gladiolas and pansies created an expansive range of color. I would find myself studying the pansy faces, finding engagement and listening to a quiet language and conversation.

My father enjoyed bringing my mother cut flowers. The garden was engaging, not only to me, but to the butterflies, hummingbirds, bees, toads and snakes as well. I would often walk there, pulled in by the contrasting faces of the flowers, from the gangling hollyhocks to the diminutive pansies, picking up random stones and throwing them at a telephone pole or a passing sparrow as I went along.

My siblings and I have carried on my father's gardening tradition. Like my father, I shepherd several flower beds—cut flower gardens and a shade garden (home to many species native to the Catskill Mountains) where I now live in Sioux City, Iowa.

My father brought the color of the gardens into the house. He had been a color expert with Pittsburgh Paints. He mixed his paint as he painted. I remember him sitting on his haunches, surrounded by paint cans, mixing and matching until he perfected the color he was applying. These were times when nothing was wasted. Dad accumulated partially used cans of paint, pouring and mixing, he could match any color. Every summer, some portion of the house needed wallpapering. It took him hours to set up the cutting board with its metal edge and sliding blade. The act of shuffling through the wallpaper books for something intricate, something appealing, cost little money. It was color that was a rich part of our lives. Money was in short supply. His eye, blending varieties of color, created a context which enriched the life of everyone in our home as well as creating a lifetime of invested interests and appreciation.

Plaster walls yielded to cracks, particularly behind the pot-bellied stove, our only source of heat for years. Preparation of the walls for painting and paper hanging was a meticulous job. As he prepared the paper to be hung, he would apply paste to the last sheet and drape it over his arm. Using a broad horsehair brush, he would work the paper into place, tapping and stroking it gently, perfectly setting the seam and the line toward the perpendicular. As I've grown older, I remember how beautiful and symmetrical his work was. He created awe as he tackled the impossible. I learned from him that work separated from drudgery created a more hospitable environment. The broken could be made whole and more beautiful.

The rich colors in my father's garden on the outside carried over into his painting and paper hanging on the inside. It was an artistic endeavor, one that brought civility as well as beauty to our humble rural mountain home.

# In the Old Man's Laughter

Seductively, wizened, glintful eyes
Interactive spider webbed network of aged lines ...
Reclusive serendipitous refractions
Time warps of intoxicating introspection

Unpretentious mischief
Disengagement from the bounds of protocol
Indulgent fruitage of a disciplined asocial perspective
Pixied unassueagable unrepentant mirth

Uncle Alton (Bud) and Aunt Elizabeth Boyce

# New England Garden

Pick ax
Crunching earth and rocks
Stones gathered up
Reappearing
Seeming to multiply

Japanese beetles
Awkwardly lifted off
Each rose petal

In the fall
Stems trimmed back severely
Each rose bush
Covered with leaves
And baskets

Some survive
The winter

# The Flowers had Sagacity

Hollyhocks flourished among the rocks and
bits of soil
On hot days, bees inspected the tier of flowers
Geranium-like leaves textured not unlike felt

Late in the summer, seed pods provided an
experience in finger dexterity
None were ever planted in some systematic way
Nor were they ever picked and painted in
bouquets

Their interminable task
Was to grow in out-of-the-way places
To punctuate the relaxed pace of country
living

# People: Deer Hunting

Deer hunting season began with the Thanksgiving holiday. November provided the dimming of nature's lights prior to the solstice curtain call. Flocks of geese mounted the winds moving southward across the Catskills along the Hudson River. In prior decades, hunting took on serious consideration, when the crops were laid away and the wood cut, with winter closing in fast, life depended on the event. The provisions for sustaining life over winter were in place. Generations of elders hunted these mountains, initiating younger folks into an intimacy with place, which later on would serve to answer the question: "Where are you from", and then even more personally; "What do you call home?"

My father began his preparation on an evening where he would break out his guns. His pistol was cracked open, each cylinder cleaned, first with a small circular wire brush, then wiped clean with a white cotton rag, finally, lightly oiled. Next his lever action rifle was opened and cleaned in much the same way. There is a set of experiences which prepare us for involvement with nature and which set the tone of a personal ethic. To my father, the hunt was a personal journey. When his guns and ammunition were laid out, he would continue the preparation by finding the hunting knife, laying out his red and black checked hunting cap, pants and jacket and dressing the high leather hunting boots with a preservative oil, an act which did not necessarily assure him of dry feet.

The morning of the hunt would begin in the darkness of time, hours before daylight. As my father began to dress, my mother would put on the coffee pot and clean the thermos, prepare a hearty breakfast of scrambled eggs, sausage, and pancakes. After pulling on the long wool socks and leather boots, he would lace his hunting knife in his belt, and then tuck his pants under the top of his socks. He gathered his deer rifle: a 30/30

Marlin Lever Action, and his .38 Special long-barreled police revolver. He carried his .38 Special bullets on his belt with 30/30 shells in his pockets. With the thermos in hand, in the darkness, my mother would hand him a small bag of hard candies, a loving act which consecrated her participation in the ritual. It was not accompanied by words. It didn't need any. She followed similar behavior when he prepared to drive a snowplow through the high passes of the Catskills in the teeth of winter storms. Now he began the short drive to Wittenberg where his climb and hunt began in earnest.

West of our home, Tawny Mountain was crowned by the Pitcairn Estate, from Old Route 28, just off our front yard. We could look up at the white buildings of the estate wondering where on the backside of the mountain, just overlooking Wittenberg, my father had slipped into seclusion. On the rocky face of the mountain, at his back, positioning himself in the hemlocks and the mountain laurel, he would do just that. Deer trails led away from him along the ledge down to the valleys, streams and wetlands.

On one particular hunt my father watched a young, short-horned (button) buck walk with his head down directly toward him. He slid the .38 from its holster and raised it above his knee, sighting carefully. As the young buck drew within 25 feet, he fired one shot and the buck fell. Dad attached his rope and prepared to drag the buck. At that instant, the doe, traveling unseen with the buck, feigned an attack. My father became concerned that he might have to shoot the doe. She snorted, stomped her feet, and charged. As he continued pulling the deer down the mountain, the doe moved along in the shadows, snorting and thrashing the bushes, airing her complete distress. This was the way of the mountain, each survivor protecting his/her own.

I remember one bow season as I slipped deep into the forest, quietly preparing a ground stand of hemlock limbs on the outer edge of a steppe, when I saw below me a red fox busily hunting a brush pile. I stopped what

I was doing and drew down on him several times with my bow. As I pulled the arrow to the release point, I suddenly saw him with a deep empathy, struck by the vibrancy of his red coat, the beauty of his form. I could not shoot.

I entered the woods as a diversion in my young life more times than could be counted. More often than not, my companion was a .22 Marlin bolt action rifle, or a simple fishing rod. With or without tools, the experience was private, impactful, and recorded somewhere in my being. Too often I was not simply alone, but lonely, and nature comforted me. Nature provides all the ways of being, sometimes an impermeable membrane, the terror, the sense of sublime, punctuating so cleanly and deeply. Most times, nature operates with permeability—awakening the senses and allowing one to create such evocative literary masterpieces as William Cullen Bryant's[1] *Inscription for the Entrance to a Wood* and Henry David Thoreau's[2] *Walden*.

There were those who did not understand the very connection to this outdoor experience. Sadly, the Catskill Mountains attracted hunters who simply came to destroy. Wendell Berry[3] stated this best in his essay, "The Risk" from his collection called *Recollected Essays* (1965-1981).

> The hunting season is open. They walk in
> these foreign places, unknown to them
> most of the year, looking for something to
> kill. They wear and carry many dollars
> worth of equipment, and go to a great deal
> of trouble, in order to kill some small
> creature they would never trouble to know
> alive, and that means little to them once they
> have killed it.

1 **William Cullen Bryant (1794-1878)** American poet and editor.
2 **Henry David Thoreau (1817-1862)** American writer, philosopher and naturalist.
3 **Wendell Berry (1934-)** American farmer, essayist, conservationist, novelist, teacher,

Many hunters come to nature with no inclinations toward a broader experience, wearing one's ego as a 30-06 hunting rifle, loaded at a sporting goods store in New York City. They crave the feeling of holding a semi-automatic weapon, wanting to kill a buck with a large rack. In some instances they buy a rack from a poacher, or from some poor mountain family who believe that an unexpected sum of $250 will greatly improve the condition of their lives, but instead this interaction diminishes the status of both.

Nature will not soften the heart of those who would despoil her for some sordid end. Killing the large buck, for some reason, has become a symbol to prove one's manliness. Now, many Americans have replaced the symbol of the gun with home buying, with owning vistas, or shoreline. Frederick Law Olmsted[4] warned of the wealthy buying up mountain tops, where democracy would be dependent upon a delicate balance between the rights of property owners and the investment of all Americans in the natural environment.

Our vistas are a natural heritage. There have to be wild places where the elements of a regional perspective are protected and where citizens can become acclimated to these vestiges of wildness and find personal attachment. In our quest for the perfect way of living, we have created the suburbs, where Americans with lesser resources do not and cannot live, where social convention is actually more exclusionary than any iron fence of a gated community, creating new ghettos of intent and undesignated "reservations".

The role of hunting is on the wane in the Catskills. When my father and I hunted, we crossed many unposted property lines. Today, land ownership in the Catskills is more and more in the hands of those who don't live there. Posting signs are epidemic, limiting the access to the

---

4 **Frederick Law Olmsted (1822-1903)** Considered the father of American landscape architecture.

vistas, streams, places to hunt, the wildness we once knew. No longer can children easily roam freely, explore, and have the opportunity to build a personal environmental ethic.

Ritual basket by Barry Hopkins

# The Eye of the Bobcat

It seems to me that when there are no
longer bobcats
The visions that pull young children
into evergreen forests
With the prints of snowshoe laces
extended out through the Princess Pine
and smallish saplings
of fresh growth,
Will have little opportunity
to find expression.

There is an extinction that precedes
the absence of the thing itself
It is known in the longing,
the pain the Plains' Indians
must have felt as the extermination
parties emptied from the trains.

There is an emptiness in this
that cannot be filled
by more civilization.

Those fortunate enough to have known
the eye of the bobcat
from some dozen feet away

Know its voice as part of their living
have forever, how brief a time,
lived.

# Resurrection

Sometime after the geese flew high
Reincarnating the cry
Of a thousand painted warriors in war bonnets
The weather sodden soil
Sucking at all that touched it
Erasing the boundaries between that which man had created
And that which emerged from the bosom of the mother earth.

Rotted leaves shrouded with decaying ice
Hung on as nature does to the passing season
If one were to inspect closely those places
Rich with loam embellished by the trekking sun
As it moved north in the assumption of its spring station
The tracks of civilization interred in the debris of time
Recorded in pieces of pottery and remnants of cold fires

As the seasons emerged from the shadow of thunderstorms
To the fast moving north winds of fall
The smell of burning wood and the falling away of darkened leaves
The moon in stark desolation
Lighting the path of Indian ponies streaked in white
As the mournful cry of prowling coyotes echoed the remorse
of the dead.

# Winter in the Mountains

Walking to the privy on starlit nights
Grasping the pump handle in the cold
Bare hands stuck to the frozen metal

Chopping wood on a massive stump
Ax caught in the gnarl of an unforgiving knot

Patches on
boots,
jeans
and socks.

Flannel sheets
Blankets piled high
Brothers huddled together
Under the blankets
For warmth

Pot bellied stove
Cats too hot to touch
Plaster crackling from the heat
Buckets of ashes

Checkered woolen caps
Pulled down with earflaps
Scarves and mittens

Under the bed
chamber pots
to be emptied
rugs to be shaken

High leather boots
heavy socks
leather laces

Ice encrusted pines
creaking
in the cold north wind
Winter in the Mountains

pencil drawing by Barry Hopkins

# People: Grandfather Gray and the Copperhead

Our mountains were commemorated by stories and folk myths which were sources of strength, fear, wisdom and mystery. When we walked to the Ashokan Reservoir to fish, my Grandfather Gray would lead the way. Departing from the Glenford Church, the only church one could depart from along our side of the Ohayo Mountain, we ambled along a well-defined path through a pine forest. Blueberries, strawberries, red mint berries lined the way as we lollygagged our way to the church cove of the Ashokan Reservoir. One attribute of my mother's immediate family, that set them apart from the religiously dedicated family members of the Glenford Church, was a fondness for mysticism. They relished the mountain folk beliefs and spirits that occupied the cliffs, trees, and hollows. Headless horsemen were a way of life, not a tall tale spun by a Connecticut Yankee.

My Grandfather Gray was a man of many talents—he raised cows, chickens, and hogs, all of which were butchered. He toiled over a very large garden of turnips, parsnips, cabbage, peas, sweet corn, and rutabagas. These were all life sustaining foods, though there were other items grown that simply assaulted the senses. It was clear to me that good tasting food wasn't always essential. He shared with many mountain families the art of raising a family by farming, fishing and hunting. The main necessity, though, for being a jack-of-all-trades was to be hired out to anyone who could afford his skills, such as those part-time "summer residents" who owned a second home in the Catskills. He was a master stone mason and to this day you can view many of his very fine stone walls.

However, it was one of his other activities that, for me, best defined his experience with the mountains and his wisdom and use of myth. One fine day, a group of us were walking from the pine grove to the church cove to go fishing as we crossed New Route 28, then went over the railroad tracks to an open glade, where the grasses grew above our knees, rubbing our bare legs, and alerting our senses. At this point my grandfather raised his arm and announced, "Stand still! Don't move! I smell a copperhead. I smell cucumbers." We froze in apprehension and fear, barely breathing.

In an earlier time, my grandfather had been laying a wall where high above his head, he felt a snake. Instinctively, he grabbed hold, quickly realizing that this what not a harmless garter snake, he yanked the serpent from its resting place and found a very large copperhead. Fear took hold as he held tight with his grip, just behind the snake's head. The snake writhed all over his arm and body. Then, with a force beyond his own comprehension, Grandfather Gray flung the snake into the nearby bushes. For some reason, at that moment, he was infused with the smell of cucumbers, an odor which he would forever associate with the presence of a copperhead.

When he lowered his arm during this fine fishing day, he relaxed. He shared again the story and how he equated the smell of cucumbers with copperheads. He spoke of the mortal fear he experienced that day, breaking out in a cold sweat and shaking. It's the only time I saw him show fear. He always trembled when he told us that story.

One lives in the mountains having a deep respect for two species of deadly snakes, the copperhead and the eastern diamondback rattlesnake. I don't know about rattlesnakes, but copperheads smelled of cucumbers. That was the plain and simple truth, according to my grandfather.

NOTE ON MY GRANDFATHER:
My grandfather, as he lay dying, carefully eyed the grief-stricken family gathered around him. Rural mountain folk pride themselves on wailing and on the very fine art of grieving, the author included. Wailing, also known as keening, is practiced in many cultures as

a means of expressing the grief of those close to the deceased. From the Lakota Indian women in the Great Plains, whose keening was heard as their men were returning from battle and the extent of their losses were understood, to Celtic women in Ireland, to rural people almost everywhere, this shared custom expresses a strong sense of cultural continuity and loss. To these sad tones my grandfather quietly commented, which was his way, "Don't cry for me. I'm the only one here who knows where he is going."

# Grandfather's Drift

He knew things that were not known,
that the smell of cucumbers
    in the tall grass
        near the path
masked a lair of the intrepid copperhead.

He contrived practical but awkward inventions…
Leaving the click on the level wind casting reel
    adding sinkers until the pole bent
        casting to the brink of eternity
with nary a snarl or backlash

He could construct a house
from discarded weathered boards,
    with joints a quarter inch apart,
        on tangent,
nailed incoherently

As he lay dying,
He continued in the usual way,
    when dry eyed
        he casually observed
the disquieting tears of those he was concerned for …

Note: It's worth noting that my Grandfather Gray, at this point, was blind.

# People: Mountain Women

Grandmothers are often portrayed as idyllic images of silver-haired goddesses, neat as a pin icons. My Grandmother Hopkins resided in a small home in Cherry Hill, southeast of the Ashokan Reservoir, in upstate New York. When Grandfather mowed the lawn, copperheads and rattlesnakes were sometimes decapitated. Grandmother Hopkins saw no reason to dispose of any snake, and so fried "chicken" would often await us at the table.

Grandmother Hopkins had her name "Pearl" tattooed on her arm. She was the mistress of her domain, which included not only the house, but her acquired avocation as a repairer of torn jeans, a seamstress extraordinaire, and shoe cobbler. I can picture her now, sitting at her cobbler's bench, carving a heavy piece of leather to replace the worn-through soles of a pair of shoes, a row of tacks in her teeth and a cobbler's hammer in her hand to finish the repairs. She wore her hair in a bun and sported wire-rimmed glasses.

Grandmother Hopkins pushed all of the traditional boundaries of child rearing, more concerned about the children that we were and not about the adults that we would become. She really was a Mother Bear, caring more about the grandchildren than the parents. She helped construct corncob pipes with corn silk, which we smoked when no parents were around. She also brewed strong cups of coffee, which we consumed with large helpings of cream and sugar. Grandmother Hopkins raised dunking to an art form. Stale bread, stale cookies, stale crackers, we were always dunking. For a child she was like having an impish gnome as your best friend, a contriver of mischief.

One day my Grandfather Hopkins lost all patience with me when I was fighting with one of my brothers, and yelled. I began to cry. As soon as he was out of earshot, Grandmother Hopkins handed me my Grandfather's favorite shotgun and a few shells with instructions on where to go. Grandmother was well aware that nothing would have been more offensive to my grandfather than for her to give me one of his guns. It was an act of defiance. The only advice she gave me was, "Be home before your Grandfather returns." What was so extraordinary about her giving me that shotgun is that Grandfather was a professional shooter, who prided himself on the quality of his guns. He was not into sharing. When he played cards, he played Solitaire, a dangling cigarette gripped in his teeth. When he and my grandmother fought, it was with rough words shot out in staccato fashion, both of them talking, no one listening.

Grandmother kept a loaded 410 single shot shotgun right inside the front door. Mountain women were forced by convention to extremes of behavior to protect themselves. Once, a traveling salesman had pushed past my Grandmother, into the house. Once the saleman was in, she eased the shotgun into his face, gave him to the count of three to clear the place, and then firmly shot him in the buttocks. (Grandmother Hopkins was not the only mountain woman in my family to shoot a man with a gun).

Grandmother was a fastidious woman. She saved every button, especially the pearl ones. The attic was a dream world of Grandmother's treasures. One rainy day we retired to the attic where she showed me a picture of a dignified Indian woman, dressed in a long black gown and glorious bonnet, sitting in a rocking chair smoking a hand crafted woodsmen's pipe. She told me the story of her great-grandfather and his Indian wife. The woman in the picture had immense dignity and a compelling presence. Like the pearl buttons, the picture was one of Grandmother's treasures, one she valued deeply.

Grandmother had a rack of bobbins filled with thread, multicolored and of various weights. When she sewed on the Singer treadle sewing machine, the air was filled with a melody claiming the effort of her day.

Grandmother baked everyday. Her oatmeal cookies set a standard which defied replication even by family members who claim to be given the recipe. Old cookies were valued to be dunked in coffee laced with milk and sugar. Tea was prepared and shared in the same way, as was hot chocolate. When she peeled her Granny Smith apples or the yellow Bavarian apples, she placed the apple below her breast cutting towards her body. In my world, nicking oneself was an everyday occurrence, and I waited for the day she would cut off a breast.

Although my grandparents slept in the same bedroom, there was very little evidence of affection between them. They rarely ventured from Cherry Hill. When they came to visit my family in Glenford Woods they did not tarry long. Their departure was always indicated when my grandfather said, "It's time to get home, time to go back to the poorhouse."

Grandmother Hopkins died of dementia. At that time, the mid-1960s, most deaths were listed as hardening of the arteries. One afternoon, as my grandfather finished a painting job, he returned home to find her missing. He searched for her most of an afternoon, finding her along the side of an old country road. She looked at him in frustration and said, "Oh Henry, where have you been? I've been looking all over for you." This was only one in a series of such episodes. She died shortly after this particular incident.

After my grandmother's death, Grandfather Hopkins appeared at our house for breakfast every Saturday and Sunday. He later began dating "younger" women who would eventually leave him for "someone closer to their age." I was with a friend one Saturday at Deanies, the local colorful bar in Woodstock, when she shared with me her disdain of the older man flirting with a younger woman at the end of the bar. She said, "Doesn't that bother you at all?"

I shook my head and simply said, "No, he's my grandfather."

Later that evening, I arrived home in time to return our car to my father who had to work. My mother was in the process of serving grandfather coffee, eggs, and pancakes. She looked at me and rolled her eyes, "I wondered which one of you boys would arrive home the latest." Grandmother Hopkins would not have been at all surprised.

# Appalachian Reflections

Lines of laundry
    Flannel shirts
    Faded jeans
    Graying socks
Drying hard
In the winter wind

Gaunt
Unshaven
Tight lipped men

Cotton dresses
Sagging breasts
Pregnant women

Food on the table
Clothes to wear
Life goes on
As it has
For generations

# Frances

Descending into the
damp bluestone cellar
she pointed out dates written
on the rough hewn beams
and the cryptic penciled notes
which recorded the history
of this community.

This town had been built
in the valley along the stream …
This town that had disappeared
with the pirating of the land
by the city of New York
to build the Ashokan Reservoir.

She understood the resolve
the hiding place
of the anger and distrust.

We worked each summer
on projects that had no beginning
or no end.
Picking up the apples where they fell,
each already in an independent
state of decay.

Pulling out the weeds from among the herbs,
Loading the wheelbarrow with rocks
where the rocks separated
bits of earth
from humus and rotted wood.

From her place in the shadow of the mountains
it was possible to view
the Ashokan Reservoir.
She led me to the cabin in the woods,
showed me the stonewalls and the meadows.

From the front porch
as thunderstorms poured through
and water descended
from the leaf-clogged eaves;
she wove the stories of this place
from the strands of families, folklore and
the hoary frost of mountain memories.

Glenford Methodist Church. Photo taken by Ashley Hopkins Benton

# People: Maggie Drew

During the early 1900s, as the city of New York was feverishly acquiring upstate property for the Ashokan Reservoir that would eventually cause the demise of many small communities, including Old Glenford Woods, the good folks of the Glenford Methodist Church struggled to procure their church building back from the city. All efforts to buy the church and move it to a new setting had been stymied. In an act of civil disobedience, akin to their Thoreauvian roots, a band of local Methodists dismantled the church one board and one beam at a time reconstructing it on the spot where Old Route 28 intersected with the Ohayo Mountain Road near Woodstock. The City of New York (which had prevailed in almost every lawsuit involving land acquisition for the Ashokan Reservoir) sued the Glenford Methodists, won, and was awarded the grand sum of less than $50. This only led to deepen the roots of distrust between the mountain folk of the Catskills and the City of New York.

Only to a small child could the rebuilt Glenford Methodist Church appear to be an imposing structure. A white clapboard church with stained glass windows which were opened in the summer to allow the sounds of the mountains in—gray squirrels, bluejays, wind, and crows. The pine grove needles shifting before the summer breezes outside the building were more compelling than the voices inside.

I remember one Sunday morning, sitting between Mr. and Mrs. Lenox, the owners of the post office and only grocery store where we lived. Mrs. Lenox showed me the flow of music and the organization of the stanzas as she taught me to sing. I stood between them, these two elders, as we sang "The Old Rugged Cross" clearly intent on personal salvation.

I soon joined the church choir, served as president of the youth fellowship, and, for awhile, harbored the dream of becoming one of the chosen few called to preach. I learned, one Easter season, that there were mountain families that constituted the core of this tiny church, (notably, many of my families relatives were members), and I became aware of the church's social labeling, the sorting and sifting of the worthies and the unworthies. Once, a man smelling of having come directly from working with his cows and pigs, was asked to leave. He never returned. My own father, a Connecticut Yankee to the core, could swear with the best of them, and except for funerals and weddings, very seldom set foot in the church.

Being saved by choir salvation, I was placed as a youth representative on the church board. One evening, while preparing for a monthly meeting, my father inquired of the agenda. I hesitated to share with him that the board was considering an eviction of a young female member from the choir. Although a long-time member of the church, it had become apparent that she was "with child" and conflicted with the very core values of the church.

My father tapped the ashes of his hand-rolled cigarette and mused, "Your aunt will be leading the committee towards dismissal, and when she does, you might want to remind her that she, too, was with child before she was married."

The minister opened the board meeting with the announcement of a pressing issue concerning a particular church member. He hesitated before continuing, and then said, "Apparently, our own Maggie Drew is pregnant, not married, and since her condition is highly visible to members of the congregation, some on the board believe that she should not be allowed to sing in the choir."

As if anointed by the Holy Ghost, my aunt unleashed a fiery tirade condemning Maggie. She acknowledged that although Maggie had been baptized in the church, and even though Maggie had been confirmed and attended church regularly, "what kind of example are we setting, if she continues to sing in the choir in her condition."

Cue taken, I spoke. "My dear aunt, my father wanted me to remind you that you, too, were with child before being married."

The Red Sea parted, as the female board members scrambled over each other in an effort to leave the church. I walked a half mile home, my heart beating victoriously, knowing I had truly unsettled things that night.

As I entered the house, the preacher was close at my heels. He grabbed a cup of coffee, sat down and said to no one in particular, "That was great ... really great."

# Maggie Drew

In the valley
Its spire reaching skyward
The symbol
Of community convictions
The church

Maggie Drew
Thirteen children
In her family
Dropped out of school
At sixth grade
So they say

Pregnant
Singing in the choir
Unmarried
A temporary condition
Here
Most people
Have to get hitched

One of God's children
Maggie Drew
Believes...
Although her mother
And many other women
Aren't so sure

Peculiar,
Only
Because they preceded Maggie
In approaching
Matrimony
This way

Older women know
That they have been forgiven
For their transgressions
And that they suffered dearly
Ensuring their deliverance

Fear grips the heart
Of many Christian women
Who in seeing Maggie
Singing so lively
In spite of her condition

Appearing to harbor
Some secret knowledge
That she might not suffer
Having to get married

What, dear God,
Will happen
If poor Maggie
Continues singing in the choir
Unmarried

Watercolor by Howard N. Horii, FAIA

# A Sense of Place:
# The One Room School

My formal schooling began when my mother delivered me to the Glenford one-room school. At that time mountain children did not attend kindergarten, so I started my "coursework" in first grade. For five years I would attend the one-room Glenford School and the two room Ashokan School in preparation for a life-changing time at a consolidated school. Paved roads, an industrialized work force and the need to "Americanize" the rural youth meant the end of rural life as I had known it.

When I began school the effects of World War II were still alive and well—patriotism and love of country were prevelent. The total class size was very large, as there were approximately 35 students in grades one through eight. The small communities prided themselves on the quality of the school and this was reflected in the addition of fluorescent lights, movable desks (not bolted to the floor), and new flooring. The previous generation also prided themselves in making sure that their children received more than an eighth grade education. Many times children repeated grades simply because they could not afford to go onto high school. Nothing was more important in my family than education, as my father had only received a third grade education, but would later in his life earn a G.E.D.

My father was an accomplished student of the "Palmer Method",[1] where penmanship was an art, not an archaic form. He had a wonderful working vocabulary, and would correct my spelling, even as I became a college student sending letters back home. Every day, I would hear the words, "You are going to graduate, and you are going to go to college." One

1 **Austin Norman Palmer (1860-1927)** American educator and publisher.

room schools treated literacy, reading, writing and spelling, as a daily collaboration. When I first entered the Glenford School, our desks were equipped with ink bottles. I developed a lifelong fascination with fountain pens. Even today, I do not compose at the computer, but freehand.

My mother was a high school graduate who loved reading, especially poetry. Because of her we knew every piece of classical children's literature. She loved to recite Longfellow's[2] "The Song of Hiawatha" to us each evening. She wrote poetry and music and instilled in us the importance of language, rhythm, and rhyme. Needless to say, my parents were very active in the school community and my father was a member of the school board and took pride in hiring what he considered to be the very best teachers. Politics often played a role in this civic center of the mountains and heated debates would occur over mountain issues and my father helped to form the Glenford-West Hurley Fire Department as a result of such debates. The country school played a very important role in the development of the communities affected by the Ashokan Reservoir project.

Country schools across the nation held ritual to the highest form. We started each day with the Pledge of Allegiance, followed by a rousing march to a John Philip Sousa[3] piece. World War II had instilled a patriotic impact— good behavior and citizenship were affirming of being American. The G.I. Bill made higher education a reality for many young men and women who had served in the military. For the two decades following World War II, these individuals were often the first in their families to graduate with a college degree. Many with military backgrounds made their way into teaching and school administration. Not all were the best candidates for the job. A few brought with them a keen reverence for order, meaning an orderly learning environment, and a controlled learning environment.

---

2 **Henry Wadsworth Longfellow (1807-1882)** American poet.

3 **John Philip Sousa (1854-1932)** American bandmaster and composer.

One cold, fall day at the Ashokan School, the fifth grade students were throwing nuts and pebbles at each other outside the school. I launched an errant throw that shattered a pane of glass on the south side of the school. The teacher was a short man, quick with his fist. He owned a punching bag inside the cloakroom. I received this teacher's fury. He slapped me several times in the face, before delivering a blow. I yelled, "Let me go, you son of a bitch." He dropped the issue. That night at dinner, this teacher, unknown to me, had been invited to share in the meal.

My mother inquired of the teacher, "How was your day at school?"

The teacher responded, not missing a beat, "It's the first time I've ever been called a son of a bitch by a pupil."

My mother didn't hesitate and without turning her head, "Bruce…"

Another incident involved the oldest boy in the classroom. After a heated exchange with the teacher, the boy announced that he was going to go home. The teacher instructed him to sit down. The boy's younger brother announced that he was going to leave too. The teacher grabbed the younger brother, slapped him around and then threw him into a chair. Corporal punishment was not against the law, and in some districts, even supported by the community. Sometimes, however, the punishment was so egregious that the teachers were asked to leave.

There was humor in the indiscretions as well. One winter a crisis developed as it was observed that the coal bin had been "picked clean"…a theft. The community assumed the thief lived nearby. The real thieves, who had buried the coal, were six and seven year old "train robbers", fantasizing about the "gold" that would buy them treasures. I didn't tell my father about the incident until I was well into my twenties, and the thieves had never been caught.

Direct instruction took place on the blackboard, and any aged child was welcomed to participate. The idea of "peer instruction", of "community-based education", and "cross-age learning" surely began in the country school. While critics of the one-room school claimed that the children lacked the intellectual development of the larger school districts, proponents, even to this day, will state that the independence in learning and the self motivation required in the country school produced students, who at the college levels, did very well. Collaborative groups were a necessity for the teacher to manage a classroom of 35 students with so many grade levels. This allowed the teacher to roam the room and provide instruction to individual pupils who needed it. As for me, it allowed a freedom to go anywhere on the school grounds for vocabulary, spelling and math practice as well as enhance my own perceptions on the value of the "walkabout."

In my third year of school, a young male teacher and his family moved a house trailer onto the school grounds. This was often allowed as part of a teaching contract. He came to exemplify the art of connecting the formal instruction with the natural environment. One snowy day he dismissed class. We spent the day rolling snowballs, very large ones. It took several students to move them into place. These became the base for an Eskimo igloo, large enough to hold the entire class. As the walls formed, slanting inward, smaller snowballs were needed until the tallest boy in the class completed the structure, setting the last ball in the hole in the roof. Every child, including the teacher's family, worked on the structure. An effort in collaboration, and a lesson in building, taught me the value of the out-of-classroom experience.

Another incident with the same teacher comes to mind. I spent several days on the Ohayo Mountain, alone, working a creek rock into a facsimile of an Iroquois hand hatchet. When the piece was finished, I carried it with me for several days, rubbing sweat into the seams, turning the hatchet black. I didn't need to explain to the teacher where I was. He knew that the critical aspects of having life's experiences, those that emanate from place, improve our learning and emotions.

—

Walks to school were sometimes social with friends, or my brothers. Sometimes they were made by msyelf, but no trip to school was ever wasted time. There were many routes to take depending on the season. We gathered leaves in the fall for pressing, or spring flowers to share with our mother and to press for later projects. We carried out snowball fights while running. The act of getting to school was part of the school curriculum. We were very physically fit. Like the Kenyans, Mexicans and Ethiopians who dominated distance running at the Olympics over the next decades, we became runners. My brothers and I continued running well into our later years.

My environmental inclinations began at home as a preschool child, but the walkabout instilled in me the true love of learning. One day the regular teacher being absent, we had a substitute. At recess, equipped with the American Veterans Association's bugle, (who held meetings at the school) we drifted into the nearby swamp. We spent the remainder of the day in conversation about the natural environment. Learning the names of the flora and fauna, I was hooked. While science played a very small part in the day to day instruction, the world outside the school created the perfect classroom for me. I saw learning as something to be part of, involved with. I wanted to read and understand nature in a way that the contained classroom avoided. I wanted the truest form of hands on, minds on, education that is, all these year later, finally being "introduced" to the educational system. My "community" existed well beyond the confines of the classroom and I became what Sylvan T. Runkel[4] referred to as a "citizen of the natural world." I grew to understand how important it was for children to know and understand the region around them before becoming an activist for something remote, like a rainforest. The art of observation and reflection became the natural process of learning.

---

4 **Sylvan T. Runkel (1906-1995)** American naturalist, teacher, conservationist, pilot, musician and co-author of wildflower guides.

As we grew older, my brother Barry and I created a process of cataloguing our thoughts through sketches, drawings and writings in personal journals. I drew from my experiences as a child, as I wrote of the places I had been. The one-room school experience created a "sensing" environment which was also fueled by Spook Rock, the pine forests and the small streams that we explored every day. Reflection and art transcended into a lifetime of writings and drawings.

The freedom I had in the one-room school was not to be replicated when schools consolidated. Although with consolidation came a great expanded set of course offerings and many individual teachers who became wonderful mentors, the larger system helped me become more familiar with the impact of community expectations and social class consciousness.

The smaller setting of the one-room school provided me with a very clear sense of community, where personal growth was enhanced by daily interactions with children of all ages. In the larger setting of the consolidated school, my sense of self-worth was often brought into question by the heightened sense of social factors such as income, travel experiences, medical attention, social standing, and educational levels of the parents. I slowly began to believe that some children were expected to learn and become advocated for, free to pursue their talents and opportunities, while other children were expected to become productive members of an industrialized workforce. One indicator of this would be the tracking systems that became predominant in all the consolidated schools across the country.

One room schools were uniquely constructed to meet the educational needs of children in rural communities. We fished to provide food for the table, we learned the plant names and identified the ones that were poisonous for survival. We examined the ponds and streams to find evidence of pollution and erosion so as to better help our elders with the day to day struggle of farming and business. We developed at a pace that met both our personal, and our community, needs.

Because of declining enrollments, because of cost efficiencies and the need for a more comprehensive educational system, one-room schools across America were closed. The community sensitivities inherent in one-room schools were immensely altered.

What did I learn from each system? An important thing I learned in the consolidated school was to question the validity of social standing and to understand the need for social activism and civil liberties which led me to write my doctoral thesis in teacher civil rights and led me to a career in education. The one-room school experience, however, left me with a sense of place, natural as well as social, and clarified the responsibilities and connections that we all have, to nature, to each other, and to the larger community. Inherent in place are those things that connect us.

# The Rules of the Game

The five and dime maker of dreams
Pearl handled pistols with double holsters tied
    at the leg
And rotating cylinders masking rolls of caps

The owner of a Hopalong Cassidy bike, with white
    walled tires
The same person whose baseball and glove belonged
    first to him
The only ball devoid of layers of tape and bat
    absent nails in its fractured handle.

There were social adjustments
A board addressed with a rip saw became a repeating
    rifle
An old bike with proper oiling and a coat of paint
    was infinitely better than no bike at all

Rye Beach could not match the thrills of grape-
    vine swings and iced sled runs
Variations on rope skipping alone and in tandem
Rocks sent skipping across placid waters

On reflection
The only thing on account
Was that if you didn't own the bat and ball
You could not call the game off and go home...

# One Room School Revisited

On the hill
Students romped as cowboys and Indians
Hiding coal
As buried gold
And taking hostages

Recess capers
Jumps, twists and turns
Around protruding rocks and trees
On the steep hillside

A short two years later,
I returned
To recapture the thrill
Of bygone hillside frolics

Down I ran,
Across the hill
Around the trees and boulders
A feeling of uneasiness enveloped me
The hill had lost its charm

I thought back
To those earlier years

The trees
the rocks
the hillside
Were all there
I could not perceive
What had changed.

# The Saga of Dick and Jane

My recollection is...
That it was a college town,
    a university town,
Where people had degrees
And ate their chicken with knives and forks

There were churches you could see
And lawns that were manicured
By people that did not live there
The street lights had civility
To turn on in the evening, and off in the morning

There were bird feeders with sunflower seeds
That served slate gray juncos, cardinals and such
The cars were undercoated
Their windows opened with a touch
Not with the obtrusive cranking of a steel handle

Leaves never rotted or were burned
They were picked up and carted off somewhere
Squirrels never crossed the street but ran high wires
The cats were neutered
There was some cohabitation, but nothing intimate

There were colored televisions and computers
In the family room in the basement near the bar
With pictures of Jesus and grandmother
Along with fraternal plaques
The family Bible and *Readers' Digest*

It was a clean town
The sanitation man wore a tuxedo and lived on the hill
Trees grew straight up
There were no TV antennas
The electrical cables were underground

People kissed without touching
Sex took place on Wednesday and Sunday
If there was no early church and the shrine did not meet
Driveways were paved
Rocks were placed where they were and painted
In the backyard pink flamingos and green porcelain frogs
Stood guard with upside down bathtubs
And a statue of the Virgin Mary
Worms came out only at night if it rained hard

People wore gray foxes
Kept guns to shoot clay pigeons and intruders
Lawn sprinklers popped out of the grass
Fertilizer kept the weeds down
There were no well worn paths just sidewalks

There were no clothes lines
Geese flew in perfect formation
Golf courses abounded
Children attended private schools
And Parcel Post seemed everywhere

Women could not have facial hair
No one served in the Army
Although everyone thought it was a good idea

Most people had a summer home
Where they went to be human and commune with nature

There were zoning ordinances
To assure that buildings looked alike
Levies to keep the water out
Bug zappers to kill the bugs
And self-help courses at the Y.M.C.A.

People washed their hands when they visited the restroom
Flossed their teeth
Flushed the toilet while they were going
And made love in bed

People went to church for the opportunity to give
To psychiatrists for their mental health
Popped pills, drank drinks, manicured their nails
And wore silk pajamas to bed

There were no Heinz 57 dogs
Or labor unions

# A Sense of Place

There are times in the early twilight of winter
When the stars appear in profusion
When the sound of the wind debates with silence
And the rustle of dried grasses serves as a notice and a reminder

Deer gather to feed in extended herds
Carrying out a communion which the threat of winter sanctifies
Rabbits in their late night dances illuminated by a new full moon
Punctuating the snowscape with their characteristic signatures
    like Beethoven's *Fifth Symphony*

Nature flirts with folks' emotions
January thaws crocuses pushing their heads through iridescent snow
Trail blazers defy the winter ending storms
Flocks of geese battling the roar of the North Wind
Redtailed hawks sequestered on singular posts

American kestrels hovering over paths of frozen earth
Anticipating the transformation of the soil by the warming sun
The appearance of moles, butterflies and grasshoppers
Fulfillment of primal memories and promises

Spring is more than a spectacle
Its rites of passage symbolizing knighthood and chivalry
Redwinged blackbirds treating each crow as if it were Darth Vadar
An evil force to be engaged in mortal combat and driven
    from the field

Senses are reviewed as from some historic hibernation

The muted grays and browns of fall punctuated by hues of vivid
greens and yellows

Nighthawks streak the sky-killdeer running helter skelter

American robins bring nature to even the unwary, as their nests
appear above door jams and in other social places


In diminutive patches of undisturbed prairie

Bordered by highways-housing developments-and human activity

The arch of life defies humankind's intrusions and
pervasive technology

Budding trees, embraced by raptured squirrels-adaptive
prairie violets

Delicate blue-eyed grasses, enhanced by the call of the chickadee
..and the assurance of an afternoon phoebe


Alone, humankind seeks to bring on order to the universe...

Where trees no longer grow in response to the baton of
nature's director.

But like the spires of a church reach ever skyward,

Drawing our attention to some celestial definition of perfection..

Colts on awkward legs, nudged by a bonded elder

Become free to cavort with butterflies and snooze wistfully in the
breath of spring clover

The twilight of civilized behavior-adolescence

Summer's magic lantern shows, heavy thunderstorms-with
chaotic fretful winds


Monarch butterflies drawn to bushes as if to pull from the
bosom of the mother earth

Her strength before continuing on their arduous quest

Prairie grasses in full adornment stating their role in natural
    history and ecology
Reds of sumacs hinting the cessation of the growing
    season and the end of summer

In full panorama like the curtain call at the end of act four
All the actors reappear in stated vignettes
Buteos like the bust of Caesar-gaze unflinching at the
    digressing sun and wisps of frost
Dried grasses and stanchions of departed flowers underline
    the beauty of life and art of decay

Each departure
Forewarned by transformed leaves-bowed in supplication
Held on to by the hearty oak or reverently surrendered by
    embattled cottonwoods
Canadas both migrate and seek shelter-defying the frigid
    grip of the arctic wind
Like so many cemetery markers, the Hills blanketed in
    white-clearly assuming an air of continuity and celebration

Pencil drawing by Barry Hopkins

# Dedication—
## Barry Hopkins 1946-2007

Having a sense of place is not just about landscape or buildings, or even just about the place itself—it is also about the people. For many of us who worked with Barry Hopkins, who walked in the woods with him, taught with him, were taught by him, who ran with him, or who were fortunate enough to call him Dad, brother, husband, and friend, it was Barry who helped shape our sense of place. Everyone who knew him also knew of his love for the Hudson River Valley, the Catskill Mountains, the Ashokan Reservoir, and the Adirondacks—all places that became a part of him. Through him, we learned how to love a place, to know and respect what each place had to offer. If you asked just about anyone who ever walked in the woods with Barry, they would tell you that he taught them the name of at least one wildflower.

Place was paramount to Barry, and he often said that his life was shaped by State Route 28, which winds its way through New York State in a "C" shape. It starts in his birthplace, Ulster County, in the environs of the Ashokan Resevoir. There, as a young child, he explored the natural world and began a lifelong quest to protect the environment. His college years took him along Route 28, through the Catskills to Oneonta, where his art and his running were nurtured and flourished. Later in life he was drawn to Route 28's winding northern end in the Adirondacks, where the lakes and the call of the loons would serve as an inspiration for his art and his dedication to the preservation of the environment.

Barry was a passionate man. He was passionate about the environment, art, civil liberties, and running, and felt that as an educator he could best share those passions with others. As a middle school art teacher for 37 years he recognized the disconnect his students had with their community and its rich natural and cultural resources. This place, tucked between the Catskill Mountains and the Hudson River, served as the inspiration for many of the artists of the Hudson River School, including Thomas Cole, who lived in Catskill and is considered the father of the movement. Barry created, "Toward a Greater Sense of Place," a program designed to help Catskill Middle School students gain an appreciation for their home. The program has grown, and remains an integral part of the educational experience. As a member of the New York State Outdoor Education Association, and the New York State Art Teachers Association he led countless workshops, hikes, and camping trips for adults. He was a resource for many museums and historic sites. As a guest and presenter at the Loess Hills Environmental Conference in Iowa, Barry taught that a sense of place was universal and knew no geographic boundaries. His work with the Greene County Council on the Arts in New York focused on the critical importance of the arts and arts education for citizens of every age. Perhaps his greatest gift was his innate ability to teach informally—walking in the woods with his children, helping friends train for races, and aiding fellow artists as they prepared for gallery shows. His passion lives on.

—Ashley Hopkins Benton

Barry Hopkins during a commemorative service for Thomas Cole.

## DR. BRUCE HOPKINS

is an environmental educator, writer and historian. His career has included teaching in Nebraska, New York and Iowa, and serving as chief administrator of an Iowa area education agency. Bruce's life now centers on helping people of all ages connect with nature, a greater sense of community, and the literature of place. He has a deep appreciation for the arts. These commitments have nourished Bruce and his wife Jeanette as they write about their roots in the Catskills and Adirondacks of New York and the Sandhills of Nebraska, and as they work in schools and environmental conferences throughout the country. He holds a bachelor's degree from Wayne State College, a master's degree from Montana State University and a doctorate from Iowa State University.

 The Ice Cube Press began publishing in 1993 to focus on how to live with the natural world and better understand how people can best live together in the communities they inhabit. Since this time, we've been recognized by a number of well-known authors, including Gary Snyder, Gene Logsdon, Wes Jackson, William Kittredge, Patricia Hampl, Jim Harrison, Annie Dillard, Kathleen Norris, Ken Burns, Richard Rhodes, Janisse Ray, Alison Deming, Michael Pollan, Michael Martone, Harriet Lerner, and Barry Lopez. We've published a number of well-known authors as well, including Mary Swander, Jim Heynen, Mary Pipher, John T. Price, Bill Holm, Carol Bly, Marvin Bell, Debra Marquart, Ted Kooser, Stephanie Mills, Bill McKibben, and Paul Gruchow. We've won several publishing awards over the last seventeen years. Check out our books at our web site, with booksellers, or at museum shops, then discover why we strive to "hear the other side."

Ice Cube Press (est. 1993)
205 N Front Street
North Liberty, Iowa 52317-9302
steve@icecubepress.com
www.icecubepress.com

from the sandhills to the highest peaks
hugs, kisses and cheers to
Fenna Marie & Laura Lee